VIOLIN

Beautiful Music to Learn by Rote

by Samuel Applebaum
Piano Accompaniment by Louis Gordon

FOREWORD

Here we have a collection of pieces that were selected for their melodic beauty and architectural simplicity, making them easy to learn by rote. They may be played as solos with piano accompaniment or played in unison with violins, violas, cellos and basses.

These pieces may be used in conjunction with the BELWIN STRING BUILDER, Book One, the APPLEBAUM STRING METHOD, Book One, the YOUNG STRING STUDENT or the beginning level of any other string method.

Two slanted lines // mean that the bow is to be lifted from the string before starting the next note.

The comma (๑) means a slight pause or breath before starting the next note. This usually occurs at the end of a phrase.

The bowings in this collection include the Détaché, the Martelé (the notes marked with dots,) and the Détaché Lancé (the notes marked with dots and dashes.)

There are two finger patterns which form the basis for the melodic construction of these pieces: The 2-3 finger pattern — and the 1-2 finger pattern.

1. D, E, F♯, G
2. D, E, F♮, G
3. A, B, C♯, D
4. A, B, C♮, D

The students' enjoyment of these melodies will be much enhanced if the dynamic marks are carefully observed.

PUBLISHED FOR:

Violin   Viola   Cello   Bass   Piano Accompaniment

Beautiful Music to Sing and Play

Play these pieces in the upper half of the bow. Play from the middle to as near the tip as possible. Use the full width of the hair with the stick above the hair. To draw a straight bow, use only the lower arm, opening and closing the elbow joint.

The 2 3 finger pattern. - Preparation

The D Major Scale.

1. I Love Music

ANONYMOUS

In moderate time

f I love mu - sic I love mu - sic

2. Mary Had A Little Lamb

TRADITIONAL

In moderate time

p – 1st time
f – 2nd time

3. A Courtly Dance

(//) – The two slanted lines mean that you are to lift the bow before playing the next note.
(⌒) – This is called a "Fermata" or a "Hold". Hold the note a bit longer.

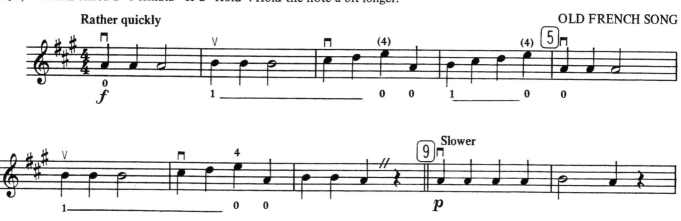

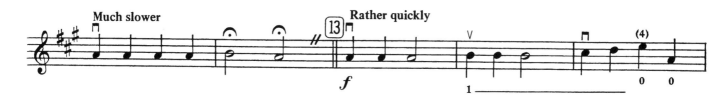

4. Lightly Row

5. The Woodpecker

The notes marked with plus signs (+) are to be plucked with the 4th finger of the left hand.

JAMAICAN FOLK SONG

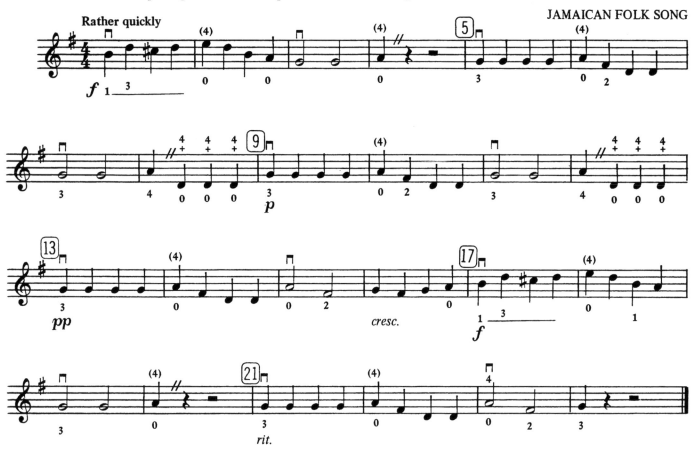

6. The Circus

The comma (❜)means a slight pause at the end of a phrase, with the bow remaining on the string.

GERMAN FOLK SONG

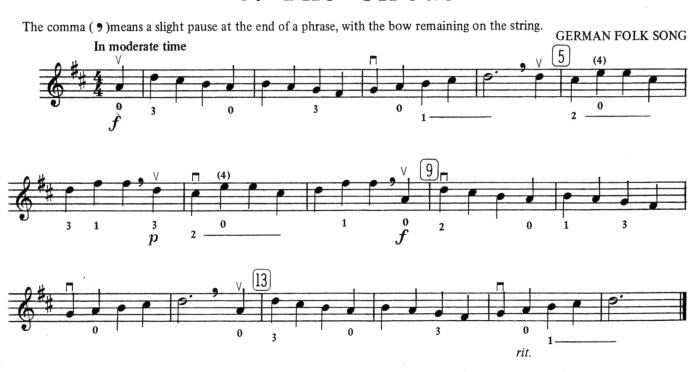

7. When Evening Brings Rest

SCOTCH FOLK SONG

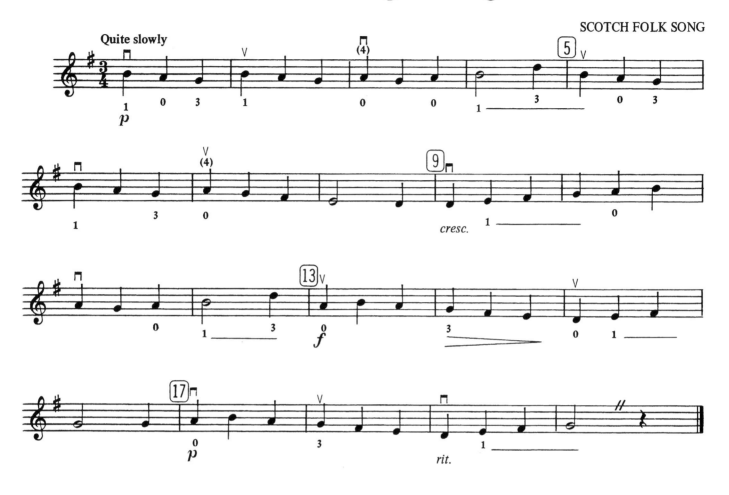

8. Good Pierrot

FRENCH FOLK SONG

9. A Merry Dance

F. WOHLFAHRT

10. Little Brown Jug

ANONYMOUS

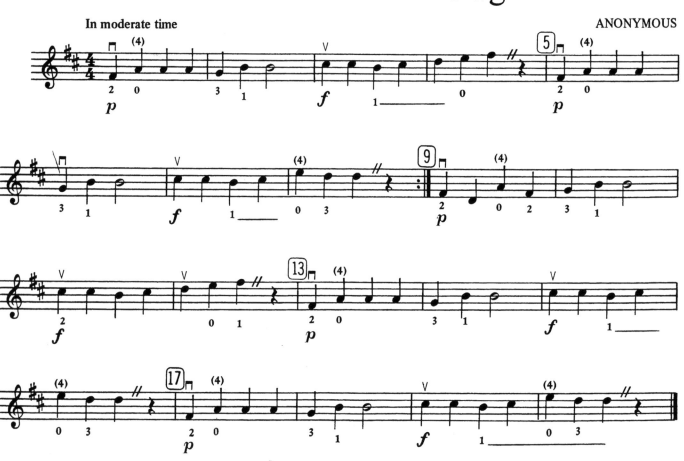

11. Loyalty

OLD AMERICAN SONG

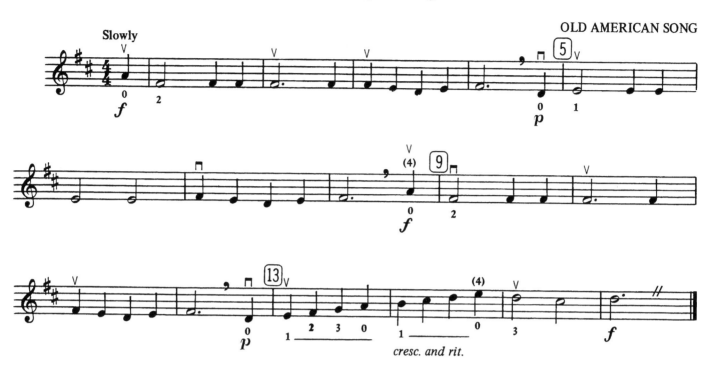

12. A Happy Thought

HENRY SMART

13. The Swan

FRENCH FOLK SONG

14. The Dance Of The Bees

PORTUGESE FOLK SONG

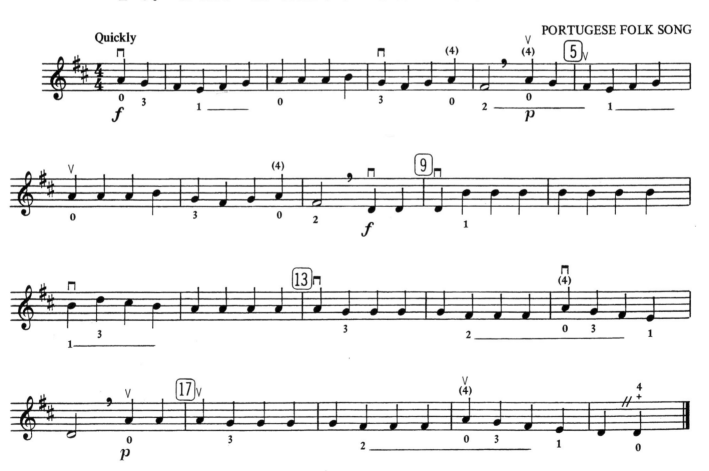

15. Twinkle, Twinkle, Little Star

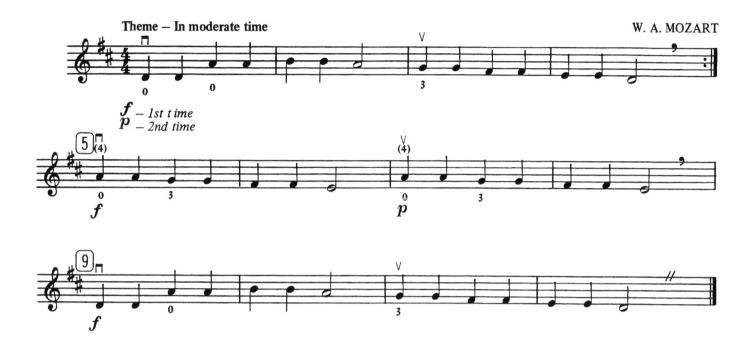

Variation

Play above the middle using the lower arm from the elbow joint.

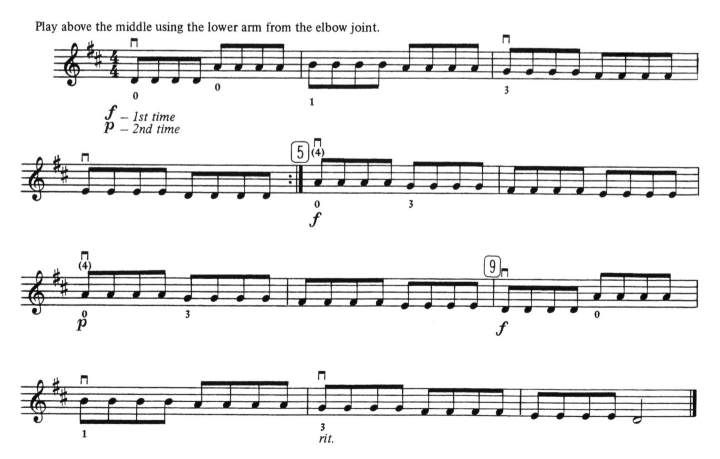

16. Melody

CARL PHILIPP EMANUEL BACH

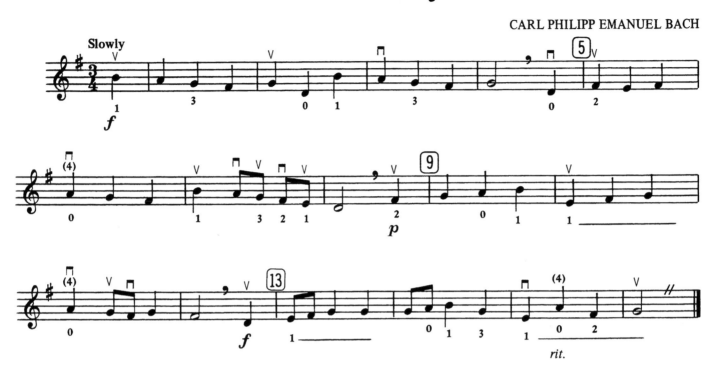

17. Find And Pick

GERMAN FOLK SONG

18. A Graceful Dance

(>) over a note means that you accent it. Accent it by drawing the bow quickly at the start of the stroke. From this page on, you may play in any part of the bow.

JOHANN C. F. BACH

19. The Old Oaken Bucket

In measures 8 and 16, the two notes are played in the same bow stroke, with a slight pause between each note.

TRADITIONAL FOLK SONG

Two Dances
20. In The Country

TRADITIONAL

21. In The Garden

TRADITIONAL

22. The Fair

EAST INDIAN FOLK TUNE

23. Short'nin' Bread

TRADITIONAL

24. The Dancing Teacher

Notes marked with dots and dashes should be played smoothly with a slight pause between each.

DANIEL G. TÜRK

25. Our Homeland

TRADITIONAL SPIRITUAL

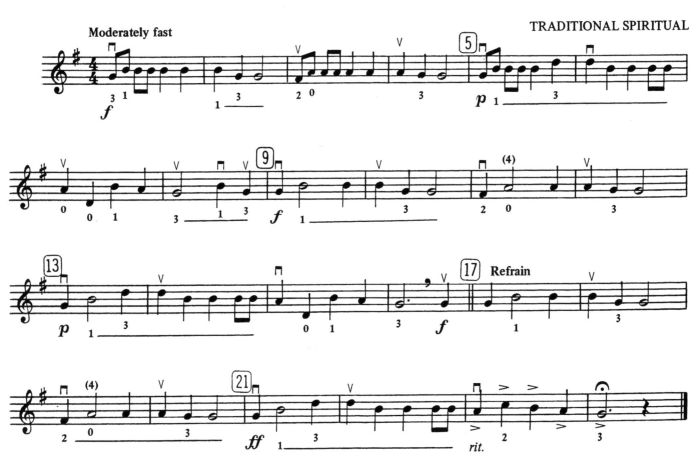

26. Fun And Frolic

A. EHMANT

Slurs-We Learn To Play Two Notes in a Bow Stroke

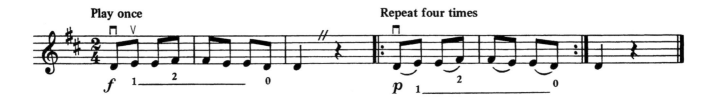

27. Thankfulness

ROBERT SCHUMANN

28. Gavotte

GEORGE F. HANDEL

Two Dances

29. The Circle Dance

SWEDEN

30. The Sunrise Dance

GERMANY

A New Finger Pattern

The 2nd finger slides back until it touches the 1st finger.

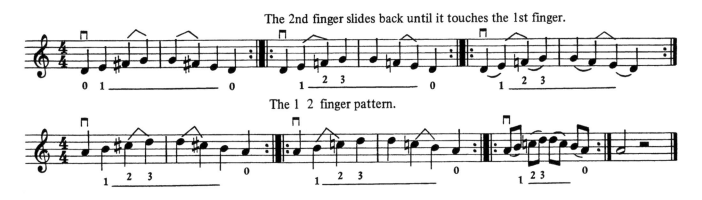

The 1 2 finger pattern.

31. The Robin

FRENCH FOLK SONG

32. The Humming Bird

GERMAN FOLK SONG

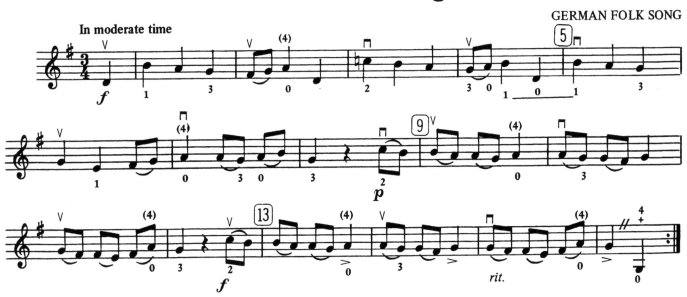

The G Major Scale

33. The Red Sarafan

RUSSIAN FOLK SONG

A New and Interesting Rhythm

Play each section four times.

34. A Conversation

MICHEL CORRETTE

35. A French Dance

F. COUPERIN

36. Auld Lang Syne

SCOTCH FOLK SONG

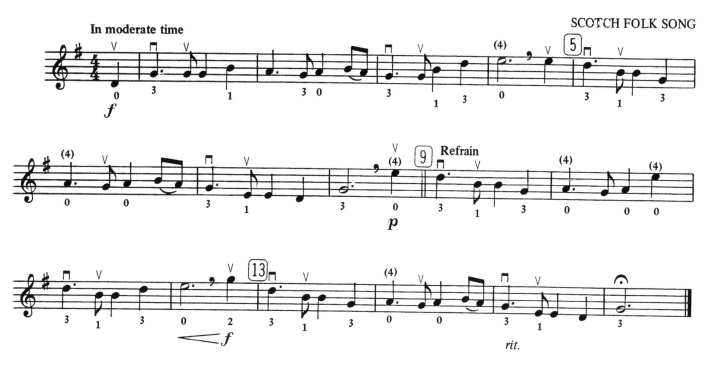

37. The Traveling Fiddler

The notes marked with dots are played with the martelé bowing. The notes marked with dots and dashes are played smoothly, but slightly shortened in length. If the left hand pizzicato notes are not played, substitute a quarter rest.

AMERICAN REEL

EL 2724

We play a dotted quarter and an eighth note in one bow.

38. America, The Beautiful

SAMUEL A. WARD

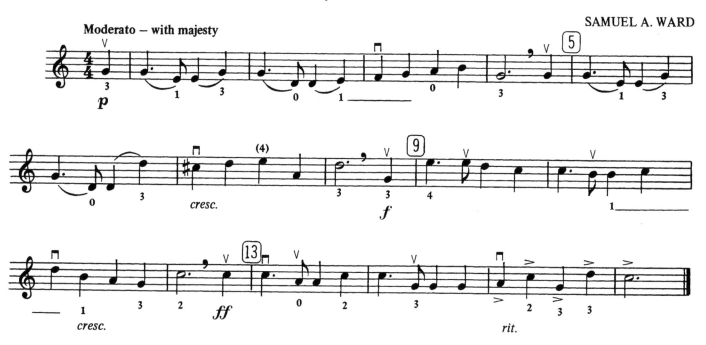

39. Hymn To Joy

LUDWIG VAN BEETHOVEN

40. Menuet

G. F. HANDEL

24

41. The Little Dustman

JOHANNES BRAHMS

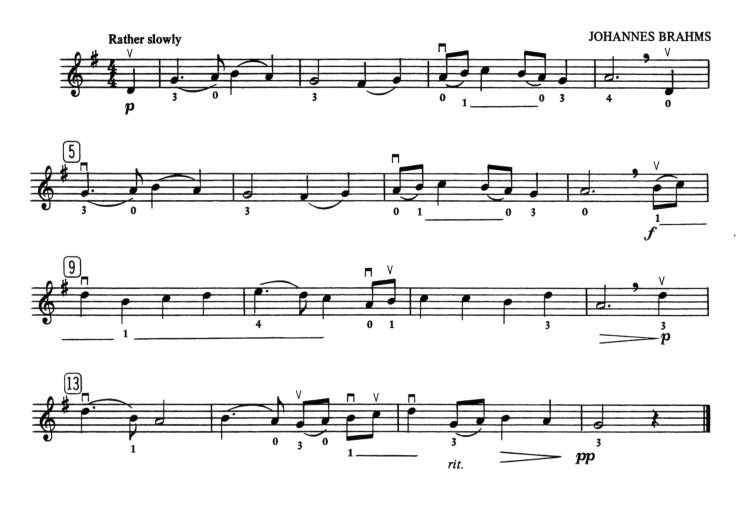

42. Allemande

JOSEPH HAYDN

43. Minuet

JOHANN SEBASTIAN BACH

44. All Through The Night

WELSH TRADITIONAL MELODY

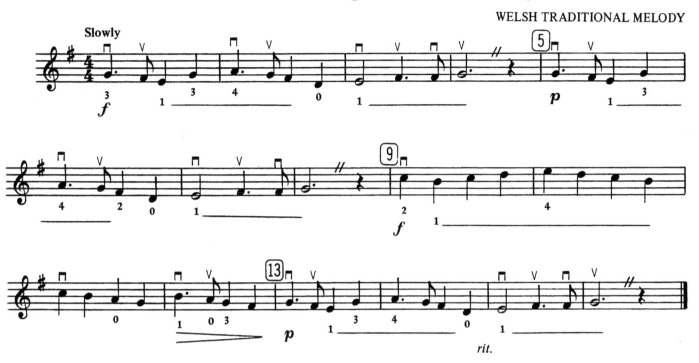

45. Austrian National Anthem

J. HAYDN

46. The Harp

IRISH FOLK SONG

47. Wandering

FRANZ SCHUBERT

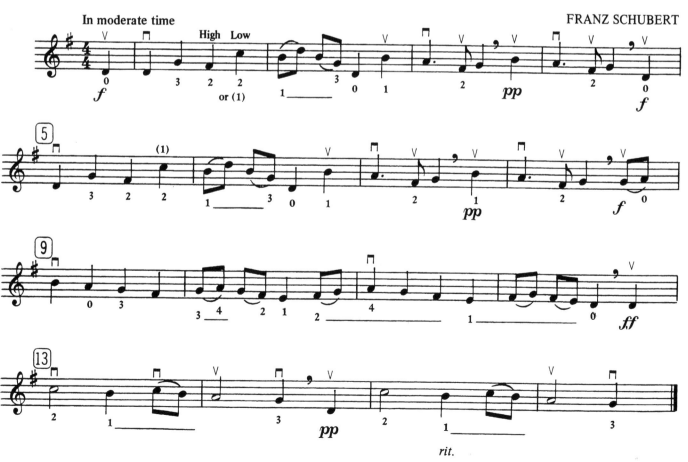

48. Suite In Two Movements

I. Bourrée

G. F. HANDEL

rit. – 2nd time

II Passepied

A Lively New Rhythm

49. Soldiers March

ROBERT SCHUMANN

A Happy New Rhythm

50. Pop Goes The Weasel

TRADITIONAL

51. The Irish Washwoman

IRISH FOLK DANCE

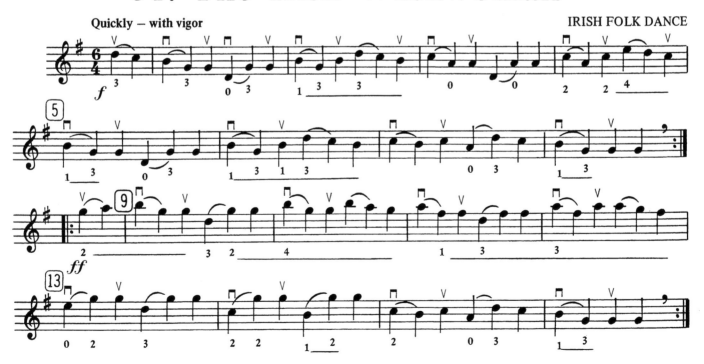

52. Country Gardens

ENGLISH FOLK SONG

53. Gavotte

JOHANN S. BACH